in dedication

strong like Jody
willful like Diana
absolute like Char
create like Tara
love like Joylynn
laugh like Trudy
speak like Caitlin
explore like Lesia
love like Vanessa

#IndianLovePoems

#IndianLovePoems

poems by
TENILLE K CAMPBELL

Garry Thomas Morse, Editor

Signature
EDITIONS

Cover design by Doowah Design.
Cover photo by sweetmoon photography.
Photo of Tenille K Campbell by Maki Fotos.

This book was printed on Ancient Forest Friendly paper.
Printed and bound in Canada by Hignell Book Printing Inc.

We acknowledge the support of The Canada Council for the Arts
and the Manitoba Arts Council for our publishing program.

Library and Archives Canada Cataloguing in Publication

Campbell, Tenille K., author
        #IndianLovePoems / Tenille K. Campbell.

Poems.
ISBN 978-1-927426-99-9 (softcover)

        I. Title. II. Title: #Indian love poems. III. Title: Hashtag
Indian love poems.

PS8605.A5494I53 2017   C811'.6   C2017-901415-3

Signature Editions
P.O. Box 206, RPO Corydon, Winnipeg, Manitoba, R3M 3S7
www.signature-editions.com

I want to believe

it all starts somewhere
these legendary love stories
these matriarchs and patriarchs
that have guided us
all into being

all love starts somewhere

let's start our love story
tonight

#2

it's an indian love affair

driving a beat-up truck
on dusty rez roads
listening to
his kid, my kid, and our kid
giggle in the backseat

johnny cash on the radio
windows rolled down
his hand holds mine
squeezes as he sings along
  tone
-deaf
but still
the sweetest time

#76

I remember your Dene lips
luscious lips
big thick lips
moose lips
that kissed your name
down my hips

I remember seeing stars
align on your cheekbones
dreams and secret wishes
just beneath tanned skin
that bore my bruised kisses
hickeys
hickeys everywhere

I remember
what you forgot

#119

I love you
my Cree lover
you and your cheek-
bones that beckon my lips
day and night

I love you
my Cree lover
the way you stake your claim
on my body
day and night

I don't love
your mother

#69

Cree Man
you are the salt and pepper
in my moose meat stew
the one i need
for spice in my life

Cree Man
you are the loudest bingo
caller in the hall
your voice echoes through the rafters
of my urbanized heart

Cree Man
i wait for you
standing behind drum circles
listening to the high twangs
calling my name

Cree Man
i wait for you
a double
double in one hand
warm fry-bread
in the other

#254

sometimes
i forget his name
when i lie beneath him
arch
  and swallow
the names of my ancestors
in the sweet rush of release
want to moan out loud
my victory
and his
but sometimes
I forget his name

#776

his lips formed
ancient sounds to beckon
loon   duck   moose
cautiously
            they all came
nose sniffing   ears flicking

you expect me to be different

calls that arched and moved
sounds that have no meaning
until directed towards you
and then
silent he could be
and still
I would come

he carried my sounds
within his body
drawing me in

now I
carry his sound
too silent
in my mouth

#204

okay I was faking
to make him feel better
moaning out loud in Dene
stuff like
esjie
dénįgha thot'įné chelekwaze
hey
that's the only Dene I remember
on short notice

pêyak nîso nisto nêwo
muttering out loud
so he knew
that he would drive me crazy
with his little *toogaloo*
tugey

I arched my back
saying things like
owieyahhhh
and *ooohhhh*
thinking
all the while
this was worth
at least two
Golden Globes

I grabbed fistfuls of pillow
screaming my latest release
rolling my eyes
as he grunted away
until his two minutes
of fame were finished

I rolled over
panting slightly
acting dizzy and giggly
kissing his lips

sëchazeh
you were the best I ever had...

esjie: oh my god/I'm so sure (slang – Dene)
dénįgha thot'įné chelekwaze: go away, white boy
(Dene, pronounced *deh-nee-gha thow-tee-nay che-lay-kwa-zay*)
pêyak nîso nisto nêwo: one two three four (Cree)
toogaloo: penis (slang – Cree/Métis/Dene)
tugey: 'fuck'/swear word (slang – Cree/Métis/Dene)
sëchazeh: my sweetie/ my babe (Dene)

#512

i am
between desire and need
and will call it love
for the ones who need
us defined

i will
slip in shadows
of bedrooms doors
cool bed sheets
moan in the dark
in a shared moment
and walk with moonlight
wondering
exactly what your name is

i taste
your sweat on my lips
your desire
in my mouth
your scent
is stained into me
and i smile
blush
remember
ache

#211

my camp husband
moans his greetings
into my neck and hair
when I welcome him
into me
when I welcome him
home

Cree from Cowessess
good with the lips
that tell me smooth lies
you are my only one
I think of you always
live with me
in Saskatoon

afterwards
he drinks tea with milk
and pulls me tight
against his chest
we listen to the tv on low
and the echo of his heart

my camp husband
mine for six nights
of inky blackness
and soaring lights
in the wild
dark
North

#43

I asked him to call me
no matter how late
so I could hear his voice

before I fall asleep
to tell me the sweet somethings
you've been texting all day

call me
so I can hear you
whisper to me
pretend
you're next to me

instead
i get text after text

sup?
u da 1
you know dis
I want you more
den my mama's bannock

when he does call
it's short
talking is too
much
it reeks of commitment

this is dating
in 2017

#28

her blonde hair tangles
with my long black strands
at midnight

they sprawl across our pillows
intertwine
slip in and out of each other
merge
until we cannot see
where we end and begin

our fingers clasp together
matching manicures
our legs wrap around each other
matching pedicures
our lips seek each other
matching lipsticks

soul mate
best mate
best friend
tinder tho

#981

sixteen and in love
walks around town
sneaks into backseats
beers by a bush fire
dark hickeys
seared onto body

lacing our fingers together
smelling of damp night air and tobacco
picking the leaves out of my hair
as you find our clothes
bathed in moonlight

neghąnighitą, you say
sëthē, I say
me too, me too

neghąnighita: I love you (Dene, pronounced *neh-gah-nee-tah*)
sëthē: me too (Dene)

#909

he was
big and black
so wide I couldn't wrap myself around him
thick and rough
but kissing me gently
as he whispered my name

he was
a blue-eyed construction worker
twenty-two with a shy grin
and he laughed
as he kissed my neck

he was
tall and slim
streamlined with beautiful lips
fed me sushi in bed
with fingers expertly
handling my desires

he was
draped over me
like a blanket of stars
his hair longer than mine
as the scent of campfire
and the low strums of country rock

now this
this is my medicine wheel

#487

he texts me late at night
lights up the shadows
in the small room
I never shared with him

i <3 u
take me bak
sorry sorry
she ain't u

it's been a year
of fighting against his expectation
of forgiveness, coming home
taking him back to our bed

three hundred and sixty-five days
of choosing me and my heart
over him and his sadness

I have cried a thousand rivers
for what was
what could have been
what should have been
I have watched the moon grow full
over and over again
watched the seasons ebb and flow

I have come full circle with the earth
using each season to connect
with the lost friends
forgotten families
and I have remembered
the stories of who I was
where I came from
and what I will be

but I don't text him back

#671

country music plays
smoke hangs in the air
fire flickers
behind
hot at my back
as his hands wander low

I play with his braids
one tooth missing but he still cute
used to powwow
took to the bottle

now he only dances in my bed

#704

hockey players
make love
like they're waiting for applause
waiting to go home
tell the story
between rounds of beer
and videogames

shaking my head
I pull him down to me
biting lips   scratching back
feeling his chest hair
scrape against my breasts
his fingers deep within me
his tongue fucking my mouth
and I smile

I mark him
biting his fingers
taste pleasure from his hand
arching my back
opening up
letting him claim
territory and privilege

he smells of sweat and sex
energy thrumming through him
as he dresses quickly
hissing as the scratches on his back
remind him of me
he's still grinning
when he creeps out the door

he has a story to share
            you know
of that Indian girl
who liked it rough and dirty
never knowing
that I've claimed my story
on his neck   back
            dick   hands
he's my story now

how does it feel?

#421

hang up the phone
she don't love you like I do
she's not on your lap
whispering in your ear
smelling of rye and coke
perfume and smoky nights
she don't love you like I do

not enough to let you go
late at night
creeping into her bed
only thinking of me

no, she won't let you do that

hang up the phone babe
let me love you

#128

your hand
slips beneath
my beading table
a short caress
a quick squeeze
you keep your eyes
averted
focusing
with a warrior's gaze
on the flickering
flat screen

never make
eye contact
you may startle
the beast
since your hands
are warm
seeking
my sacred
womanhood

spill my beads
imagine them
scattering
across the floor
as your body
disappears
into mine

#890

we first kissed
behind the closed door
at our grandma's house
wood stove burning
hot at my back
hot like hell
for my kissing
cousin sin

how could I resist
his good looks

so much like mine

#842

he loved me so
like a woman loves dry meat
thick with butter and salt
licking from her fingers
the taste of success
feast
and flesh

now
he loves her so
like a wolf
who licks the fallen moose
licking deep into body
fulfilling blood lust
shoulder to shoulder
with other
hunters

too bad
he not the only one
licking

#408

his shoulders ripple
from pulling canoe
cutting water with technique
built into him from time immemorial

he comes from ocean family
water people
he grew up in a cedar canoe
played with the salmon
learned to listen to
          every wave

how I watch him
mainlander dene
seeking that
island-bound
indigenous love

I want
to introduce him
to my lands and stories
to share with him
my traditions and secrets

but
as he passes me
his dark eyes meeting mine
a small grin on his face
I blush
look away
from a lake that
carries his stories and home and families
and all the charm of a two-headed sea-snake
and let him paddle on

some men
belong to the water

#11

he grew a beard
this cowasses man of mine
nêhiyew thinks
he looks suave
like fancy suave men
smoking thick cigars
luscious moose lips
lost
beneath the bush
on his face

his face beaver
ha

this man of mine
looks like a talking vagina
pink tongue
moist and wet
in a forest of dark bush
thick and unruly
wild and untamed

I almost feel like a lesbian
when we kiss

for him,
I'd eat his beaver

so long as he eats mine

#807

the snow fell
light white flakes
melting on contact
fading away
like old stories
after dawn

the country twang
of heartache and loss
white noise
background
as I listened
to your heartbeat
echoing my own

my hand in yours
we swayed back and forth
under street light
moonlight
memories

I need a woman like you, you said
I'll eat you alive, I said

#814

you held me close
two-stepping across the affect-laden floor
smelling of smoke and whiskey shots
my head rested against your chest
my hand entwined in yours
as the laughter of drunk
twenty-one-year-olds
floated around us

you were holding me tight
chest to chest
smiling as you guided me through
a wade of memories
one step
two step
one step
two step

your waist-length braid
streaked with silver
your pale blue eyes
creased with laugh lines
had many onlookerrs
but you stared down at me
and I smiled

cree boy, you make my heart
wanna sing powwow
on this honky-tonk
floor of sorrows

#47

he was my first
   discovery
my
 blond-haired
 blue-eyed
lover

I felt like Christopher Columbus
blazing new trails down his body
discovering his peaks and valleys
with my lips and tongue and taste
claiming it as
mine
mine
mine

signing treaty with
a hickey seared onto skin
that would fade over time
but my interpretation
of his ceding up
would be
forever
remembered
as con-
sensual

#12

she's got a bannock bum
flat and lean
yet fluffy and thick
Cree woman of my heart
sidestepping into my view
bannock bum a-swaying
my heart a-racing

the drum swings deep
her knees bend low
her long lovely back and upper thigh contract
my heart swoons
a war cry echoes for her
for that bannock bum
that sways away
to the beat of the drum

#682

He came from the South
long braid flashing in the sun
as he fancy danced into my heart
and into my bed

Dakota Nakoda Lakota
maybe even Saulteaux
his southern language
making my Dene tongue
form exotic syllables
teaching me his language
he whispered words
of his ancestors
into my mouth
across my neck
down my hips

He would sing me love songs
beats formed from a hand drum
he had made himself
at his Grandfather's knee
Ancient powwow cries
tumbled us down
to nights spent *not sleeping*
creating our own tribal music

I would cover his mouth with my hand
laughing and free as I rode him
like he would ride a war pony
covering his own nicker
of surrender and pleasure
night sky above me
wild grass below me
him within me

sweat would dry against my skin
as I lay down beside him
watching his lips
whisper thanks to the Creator
who gave us this instance
of cultural unity

I laughed then
curling up against him
sniffing at his neck
playing with his long black strands
that mixed with mine

My Saulteaux warrior
My Nakota Fancy Dancer
My Indian Lover

for tonight, anyway

#29

you burned my fry bread
distracted me with sweet kisses
that lead to us making love on the couch
while oil sizzled under fleshy dough
browned to a crisp
hardening too fast
no longer
delicious and moist

we sprang apart
hearts racing
hands covering
our mouths
we shrieked with laughter
fire alarm blazing
eyes stung
by grease smoke

now
when I make fry bread
I grin
and think of you
as the pale flesh swells
and browns
moist and hot
once again

#5

under the yellow street light
the buzzing of mosquitos in the air
dust on my shoes
the echoing sting of a slap
marking his cheek
burning my hand

then body
heat seeping through
hands under his shirt
pulling him closer
tighter
faster
his hands in my hair
pulling me up
lips teeth tongue
just a few bites
to mark territory

making out with the ex
had its moments
when you no longer wonder
what his girlfriend will think

#2001

broken Cree words
whisper down my body
between my legs
into my universe
where you tell me stories
with tongue and lips
and I take
tradition into me
until I burst

I feel invincible
almighty and woman
with legs splayed
letting him see
what pleasure looks like
without shame

this is what my ancestors
must have felt like

come to me again
my gifted Cree man
taste your language
on my skin
in my pleasure
make me moan
in those forgotten
syllables

make me
speak pleasure
once again

#68

after midnight
the moon's highlights are low
doors open for you
sit down take off your coat relax
let's listen to some music
the newest tribe
called red fills the room
low deep rhythmic
like I want us to be

your cheekbones
remind me of love stories
from the prairies of the south
and your lips...
those lips could make me Cree
I'm pretty sure

the night lingers on
as we
exchange pedigrees
your family your ambitions your hockey your travels
your sisters your son your goals your dreams your life
yes we are now up to date

I don't need your name, baby
I don't need to know who your *Kokum* is
I don't need your treaty status
I don't need your story

I need your lips, showing me new ways to speak love
I need your hips, guiding deep and dark within
I need your teeth on my neck
kissing away the pain in the next instant

ę́ ę́ tâpwe
stop   talking

Kokum: Grandmother (Cree)
ę́: yes/truth (Dene, pronounced *ehh*)
tâpwe: it is true (Cree)

#45

dene love
is low and rough
and made of moonlight
sliding across boreal floors
constant shivers
of water running over
           smooth rock

dene love
is untamed yet gentle
a piece of forever
a legend of its own
remember that time...

dene love
is pressed up against stall doors
in the shadows
laughing low into his neck
so you don't get caught

dene love
is hard and furious
rapids
a river that never freezes
the steam rising from a den
hidden in earth

dene love
is a hickey
beneath your breast
marked but hidden
his but not

dene love
is a sudden bloom
of wild rose hips
small ripe strawberries
a feast for those
who know
where to look

#14

you
you are the only one
the one I hunt moose for
the one whose beaver I skin

you
you are the only one
I hear
    across bingo halls
and powwow grounds
and I smell your bannock
when I close my eyes
it leads me to you

you
you are my winter bear
the one I sleep the seasons away with
you are my leading goose
guiding me to light and warmth

you
you are my northern lights
guiding me home
my only sweetie
in spite of
what your cousin said
don't trust him
he's just jealous you won me
blackout style

#1608

his arms wrap around me
thick and strong
skin shining white
like the moon above us
his pale chest hair
tickles my breasts
making me itchy
making me aware

he's my first
this john smith
first *môniyas* to grace my bed
to slide up along my body
and claim me and mine
just like his ancestors

he calls me wild
lets me ride until
my thighs ache
and he explodes
pulling my hair and kissing
with teeth and tongue and lips
shouting love words
as I straddle him
gazing down
at conquered goods

#32

warrior to my maiden
the one who makes me victory cry
as we ride to freedom

he speaks low and rough
nêhiyawêwin
run down my spine

my dene tongue licks
my thick lips kiss
a body that once
would have been
banned from mine
remembering that time
when our people warred
and I feel like a traitor
only the good kind
no
the best kind

he calls me
nîcimos sweetie and *mine*
I moan his name
just for tonight
in bed and in the dark
where he can't see my eyes
when I smooth over

old
wounds

nêhiyawêwin: Cree language/Cree words (Cree)
nîcimos: my sweetie (Cree)

#56

I miss the days
of back-seat hickeys
trying to find
a place to fuck
not underneath trees and skies
stark naked for the northern lights

I miss the days
of meeting grandparents
holding hands under the table
through bannock and butter
through awkward family dinners

I miss the days
of seeing a guy
across a muchmusic dance floor
and swaying my hips
just a little bit more
a circle of cousin
making me a star
his north star

I miss
innocence
fearless sex
pursuing
being pursued

#687

call me chief
he says
lightly slapping my ass
as he bends me over
band hall desk
papers scatter
         down
yearly financials
welfare cheques
education pleas

call me chief
he hisses
grunting low and hard
as he pounds deep
from his mind
        slips
old houses
unpaved roads
teachers who quit

call me chief
he moans
when I take him in my mouth
sucking hard and fast
as he grips my hair
dried sweet grass crumbling
smudge bowls abandoned
upon split bookcases

call
me
chief

#9

medicine wheel love
medicine wheel lust
chasing down the colours
of the earth
pinning them down
wherever you can
whenever you can

write me a black love poem
she asks
write about that one time
with that one guy
Jamal or Jared or Jaxon
whatever
and how he wrecked you

and I blush
and laugh
and tell the story

ever fuck a white guy
a friend had once asked
wanting to be the first
to tread upon native lands
and I remember
that one Métis guy
who was more *môniyas* than Cree
chest hair so thick
it was like a bear rug
rubbing against my breasts
but I tell him
never
and let him be the first

I'm curious about
our Asian cousins
they look so Dene to me
an honouring of my northern stories
a remembrance
and I imagine
that if I could find one tall enough
he and I could make
beautiful moments together

but
whaa whaa
no one will ever take the place
of the Red in my life
the Dene the Cree
the Saulteaux Nakoda Lakota and Dakota
the Anishinaabe the Stó:lō
the Dogrib and the Squamish
the Mi'kmaq and the Métis
the language that we speak
the secrets we carry
the traditions you burn onto my body
the way you make your fry bread

môniyas: white person (Cree)

#2000

his Métis lips
told me half-truths
that he totally believed
so it wasn't really lies

on sheets that smell of sex
listening to party sounds
outside the door
laughter booming and loud

we speak softly
nîcimos
ê
tâpwê
and we laugh
because our Cree
sucks

I use fancy terms
like *decolonization* and *theoretical discourse*
and he nods   smiles   doesn't understand
him and me
we are better silent
biting sucking licking
better than talking

half-breed and pale-breed
in love
for a fraction
of history

#96

between conversations
Indigenous politics
and who screwed who
I fell in lust
with a structured jawline
a messy man bun
and ideas too big
for Indian Act policies

he came from the south
Cree as can be
those eyes those lips...mmm those lips
he told sweet stories
made of bannock and honey
made me believe
in his Indigenizing dream
made me
want to make him a little more Dene
sign treaties
make agreements
trade moose meat and fish
for a night of wicked relations

but I walk away
shaking my head
blowing a kiss
he's the marrying kind
that Cree man
white buffalo
looking for forever
kind of romance

I'm just looking
for tonight's
            feast

#92

I fell in love at the bar
with a man whose name
I didn't even know
took him home
into my bed
played his body
like a drum
let him moan
deep and low
when he began to whisper
things he would like to do
to his little indian princess

he slept soundly
as I slowly crawled out of bed
laughing to myself
as I pondered
the age-old question

how the fuck
do I get him out of here?

#425

He's called Chief
in council rooms
in bedrooms

he sweeps in
tosses his braid aside
and dominates

asking to be spanked
by the soft glow
of candlelight

he uses words like
requisition and
unattainable

follows up with whispers
Naughty girl
who's your Chief?

He makes them beg
for access to our traditional
lands and territory

I make him beg
for my traditional lands
and territory

He seals deals
shaking hands with millions
of dollars flowing

in between my thighs
buried deep in agreements
I whisper
        Who's your Chief?

#79

I love you
he said
neghąnighitą
he said

we lay in the basement
of his mom's house
Canadian flag in the window
music on low
country rock barely heard
between sweet Dene
nothings

you're my moon
he said
the one who guides me home
he said

he let me trace the tattoos on his arm
carved one drunken night
the kind with too many cousins
too many bottles of rye
the kind where you black
out the name of an
ex on his uhmmmm
arm

I want to make Dene babies with you
he said
and bring moose meat home to you
he said

seductively, I lean in
start to gently suck
biting him
just the way he likes
never letting him know
that his cousin
whispered the same exact thing
last week

#145

northern lights
and smoky campfires
filled his eyes
whenever he looked at me

on those nights
spent cuddling
in sleeping bags
giggling
in the dark
as frozen hands
and feet touched
and...warmed up

I would get up first
make the fire
start the tea
warm up the frying pan

and eventually
he would emerge
like a grizzly bear
hair everywhere
mouth stinky
and still
he would kiss me
like it had been forever

camp love
on rocky shield grounds
beneath the evergreens

#124

mixed-blood baby boy
you are like two checkboxes in one
getting my exotic on
getting my traditional on
best of both worlds
without stepping on any toes

you take me out to reggae clubs
dance all night
shake your hips
sweat dripping down your back
slick in my hands
even later that same night

next day holding hands
at the powwow
stepping in with the beat
of mother earth
we hear whistles of
honour in the rafters
I forget
sometimes
that you are mixed
that your deep chocolate
is more brown than red
I forget
sometimes

but you remind me
night after night
with dirty talk
more urban than rez

#170

you talk big
like a hunter of old
like the moose
was *thissssss big*
the buffalo
ran like the wind
but I was faster
stronger
smoother

you know
when it comes right down to it
you shiver and shake
like a scared mouse
a blind bat
a beaver
without a tail

you fear me
me and my wildness
my strength
my laughter
that is heard across bingo halls
and powwow trails
my beauty
my lips that
are famous in their own right
you fear me
and shiver
when I step into the room

come, my hunter
my warrior
my smooth talker
with this quarry
you've more than
met your match

#258

you may be my favourite mistake
the one I should have steered clear of
the one whose name
will never be uttered again

you were a whim
a taste
that never went away
despite your twelve-week
ten-step deal in rehab
and those charges
that were a total fake anyways

those neck tattoos are real
though I picture
my name inked
permanently into your flesh
the way you taste
impresses my mouth

you promise me moose meat
and a trip to meet your family
and I laugh
because
we will
never
ever
be that couple

instead
after the dark has fallen
and before dawn has risen
we forget
for a couple hours at least
that a PhD student
and a gangster from the city
can only form
a short story

#7

the only *neechie* I know
who rocks the man bun
         instead of a braid
with casual effortlessness
saunters through campus
across the grassy plains of yesterday
using words like
indigenous worldviews and
decolonization of pedagogical concerns
and I want

I just *want*

to make him stutter through a sentence
to make him ache
to make him forget
what he has learned
to go by instinct only
instinct that will drive us
under the covers and into the dark
for the winter
decolonizing our own worldviews
as we make treaty
Cree to Dene
nêhiyaw to *dënesųłiné*

make treaty with me...

neechie: friend (slang – Cree)
nêhiyaw: Cree person (Cree)
Dënesųłiné: the people (how the Dene refer to themselves)

#3

I told you
through texts
and winky faces
that I like
your lips

they remind me
of nights spent
kissing dene lovers
campfire smoke lingering in the air
the smell of the earth
as the dawn roused us

your lips
and mine
instant attraction
no retraction
and I laughed
with delight
when you replied
do you like this?
and showed me
exactly how   happy
my comment made you

all three inches of HAPPY

wtf man wtf you had it all tall cute funny those lips that smile the at-
traction was there and I could imagine if I did want to imagine a life of
beautiful dene babies running around brown and tanned like you and
maybe another daughter pale and snow white like me and a life spent
cutting wood frying fish and hunting moose. we would have been happy
you and me and I could have spent northern light nights discovering
your body and discovering your secrets and marking you as *mine*

and now
the things that are wrong with you
can be summed up

in three little
inches

that's cute

#67

I walked up to him
claimed my space
in his eyes
at his table
in his bed

nights were spent
silent about the future
but loud in *not talking*
relating only
with roaming hands
with tasting tongues
with swollen lips

gotta love camp life

#89

making love with a white boy
still feels like treason
no matter how nice his pale flesh
looks next to mine
shadows and light
right and wrong
colonized and decolonized
making love within indian acts
and treaty lands
making love with dreamcatchers above us
mink blankets below us
invisible barriers between us
moaning in Cree
your thin *môniyas* lips
kissing my neck

closing my eyes
I could almost pretend
that your hands are rough with work
that your shoulders know
how to move a moose
that your knees
have knelt in mossy grounds
that your fingers
have plucked wild feathers off mallards

closing my eyes
all I see is brown

#9

So I make mistakes
deliberately
choosing the bad
the naughty
the ones who grin tonight
and don't remember my name
the ones who make my knees shake
and my lips curl in satisfaction
the ones who make me *feel*
for once

so what
if that white boy makes me roll my eyes
as he calls me his indian princess in bed
or if that black guy fits his own stereotypes
rap in the background and smoking ganja
as I stroke his...*ego*

So I make mistakes
owning my actions
drinking up each story
loving the laughter
emerging reborn
in my own sexuality
recognizing my own desires
learning new ways
of achieving a momentary lapse in time

intimacy arrives
looking into his eyes
not giving a fuck about tomorrow
makes me love
that much harder faster stronger wilder
until he walks away
my scent on his lips
my taste in his mouth
lingers in his mind
as long as the scratches
          linger on his body

#106

foreplay is
flinging words like
white privilege and awareness
misunderstanding and ignorance
between us
sipping on beers
running fingers
down your bare back

touching upon social matters
you blatantly ignoring
stating "everyone is equal"
or "I don't see race"
until I roll my eyes
educate you
let your tongue
enter my mouth
let you kiss
away my irritation

louder we yell
pulling each other closer
hands clench teeth bite
until I forget
you have no idea
of the position you hold
you have no idea
why I have a feather tattoo
you don't have the first clue
about butter and dry meat

I forget
while we try
our hand at
reconciliation

#187

we spent nights
between sheets   giggling
our laughter echoing off empty walls
through darkness
we kissed and licked
moaned and forgot names
calling out baby and daddy instead
giving each other
fantasies and dreams
with naughty nicknames
spankings, nibbles

with dawn
came the hangover and the grins
the searching for leftover bruises
from a night that was too good
dealing with daylight, we craved
root beer lime and crush slushies
hangover nectar of the gods that is
and I looked at you
and you smiled at me
your blue eyes warm and happy

whoa...
I had never seen you in the light before
you're white?

#231

I write these love poems
for the young women
who get their first kiss
behind the house of their best friend
who get their first kiss
on dusty rez roads
the laughter of their cousins hanging in the air

I write these love poems
for the ladies doing masters
who fall in love with the jailbird
for the ladies at home with a kid on their hip
while baby daddy still plays like he's
still the star of the basketball team
for the ladies who work all night
and go home to cuddle up
with their man just starting his day

I write these love poems
for the women who have fucked
in bathrooms cars trucks
elevators movie theatres
for the women
who have shared intimate feelings
only in bedrooms behind closed doors
for the women
who still wait for the one
passed down by oral stories

I write these love poems
for the women who love the soft shapes of women
for the men who look at their men and grin
that meaningful powwow grin
for the ones who carry two-spirits
for the ones who love everyone

#348

late night spankings
bite marks and hickeys
hidden beneath our clothes

you rocked my world
you sneaky *môniyas* you
with scruffy beard and chest hair
making me forget
how unnatural you are

I let your beard tickle my face
I let your beard tickle my thighs
I let your hands wander high
I let your hands wander low
I watched the dreamcatcher above my bed
as you made me believe
in cross-cultural
harmony
and I thanked the Creator
for such enlightenment

hiy hiy

hiy hiy: give thanks (Cree)

#675

you let me use you
let me forget your name
let me moan *baby* instead
let me bite you   suck you   sweat over you
while I rode hard and forgot
my name place situation ambition dreams life
and just felt
   wet

and for that

I would make you fry bread at night
let you drizzle golden syrup on me
let you lick sugar from skin
let you feed me fluffy bites
dipped in the sweetness
running down my body

Yasssss
I would let you eat
my indian taco
for the rest of our lives
let you feast
upon tradition
buried between my thighs
let you taste me   worship me   love me

until the golden sun
lights up the room
leaving us
only heavy breathing
and deep sighs

then I remember who I am
and who you are not

#398

he was
my best friend's ex
the one who made her cry
made her laugh
made her crazy

he was
sitting in the first light of morning
smoking a cigarette
watching me
with those dark eyes
that had once watched her

no good
he was
living in his mom's basement
driving on two spares
drinking cheap beer
and watching me
the way a wolf watches
wounded deer

the chill of late august
hung in the air
as he put his arm around me
and leaned down
nose to nose
almost lip to lip

I'm going to kiss you

I waited
a moment frozen
in a field of northern Saskatchewan
lost in the golden light of dawn
fading shadows and rising mist

then I glanced up at his closed eyes
laughed and leaned back

not today, baby
not today

#484

my first
môniyas
was everything a
môniyas should be
blond
blue-eyed
with five o'clock shadow
and that
v-
you know that v-
a treasure map
on pale
        pale lands

my first *môniyas*
was everything
I knew a *môniyas* would be
he held me close
rubbing his fingertips down my back
to the "curve" on my
bannock bum
speaking sweet love words

"Do you know how to
make a dreamcatcher?"

"Do you get
cheap smokes?"

"I knew an Indian once. Paul Seesequasis...
Do you know Paul Seesequasis?"

my first *môniyas*
he left at dawn
sharing sacred tobacco on my lands
making promises he never meant to keep

I smiled
and nodded
because his proud name
escaped me

playing Pocahontas for one night
was plenty

#6

me and him
and him
make love on the living room floor
listen to rap music
the smell of rye and coke on his breath
as he kisses my neck
while his cousin massages my back

they brown
but Real Indian brown
and I feel both
at home and slightly exotic
watching them seduce me
analyzing their movements
amid waves of pleasure

Alpha has lips
that quiver and wait to be kissed
an ego to match his body
tight and hot and hard
rippled down into a six-pack
flexing as he shifts position
pulling me into him

Beta is long and lean
a pleaser
taking cues from my moans
and Alpha's sage advice
courteous he is
when he watches me
pleasure someone else
patiently waiting his turn

        in
between
profane lyrics and laughter
sex exploration and food delivery
we discuss the politics of being Brown
the hierarchy of pale skin
and the general lack
of spiciness everywhere

the sun has touched the sky
when I emerge   hair messy   make
                                up gone
fingers intertwined with Alpha's
he pulls me tight against him
making my body remember his
leans in with one last kiss
sharing breath and smiles
without shame
as Beta waves shyly
from the living room window

#506

shushwap love
smooth jawline
and green eyes
exotic enough
to arrest interest
to confer status on future babies

he walked along
rude and arrogant
making me laugh out loud
head tossed back
chilling in sketchy five corners
smoking with drunks on the sidewalk
learning stories from the non-familial
the forgotten
the unwanted

history is history
and we aren't all elders

we ended up in an abandoned field
wildflowers brushing our knees
sunset kissing mountaintops
mist entering valley
he leans down
kisses my lips
at the cusp of dusk

shushwap love
west coast lust
whaa whaa

#809

West Coast desire
tastes like fresh smoked salmon
or maybe halibut cheeks
hot and slightly oily
settling within
like a delicious piece of
culture land tradition

It feels like coming home
wrapping myself around
arms built strong from
pulling cedar canoe
chest slim and straight
feet tied to the land
but pointing toward
         river pathways

The drum beat is low and steady
the voice comes in deep
claims your heart
with soul and song within
making me remember
the moans you would make in bed
as I taught you Dene love songs

A Stó:lō serenade
between boreal lips
within salty mouth
making love under cedars
         beside the flowing river
even though
even though
I don't come from a canoeing family

#783

long northern nights
are spent investigating his body
Dene from fond du lac
the land of moose   whitefish
men who lie and cheat and steal
the hearts of women from all around

he's twenty-four
Indigenous as fuck and 6'4"
with eyes like black shadows
and lips full and plump
ripe wild raspberries
    no wonder he has
    women howling like coyotes

he's wild that one
there's no shame in his sex game
making me do things I said I would never do
he only has to
kiss his way up my legs
bless my sacred womanhood
with lip and tongue and lust
and I will promise him anything

I make him fry bread
to eat off my breasts
nipples dipped in syrup
letting him feast upon me
within me
turning me inside out
moaning only his name
never letting myself remember
who I am without him

I'm lost in his traditional lands
in a well-worn hideaway bed
in a basement with blanket curtains
bathed in the glow of a game show
moaning into his shoulder
so his family doesn't hear me

I'm lost in the wilderness
with a man who makes me
moan in *dënesųłiné*
and melt in fond du lac

#414

you came to me in a dream
and I remembered who I was supposed to be
you showed me the drum
and sang me songs
I couldn't understand
but knew from way back when

you were my other half
if I believed in such things
but too far in the past
to be relevant to who
I needed you to be now

or maybe
you were there
to remind me
it's okay to be traditional
to sing with my voice
to beat the drum with my hand
to connect

you stalked
my dreams
with stealth
with moose meat and a song in hand
with stories and culture
and language and community

waiting for me

right where I left you

#1917

I never realized how Indian I was
until I started messing around
with non-native guys

You try to explain
why they can't put their sunglasses
on your smudging altar

awkward

telling them not to touch your feather
...not that feather, yo'...
the eagle feather that you smudge with
beaded and tied with ribbons
given to you by your grandmother

You try to explain
why you have ten pillows
seven coverlets
and five mink blankets
when you live alone
they don't understand
how many cousins you have

When they kiss you
holding you close
and their five o-clock shadow tickles your cheeks
you come to the realization
...they have body hair...

speed dating
non-indigenous
it can be quite
the commitment

#782

you slammed into me
doggy style hair pulling neck biting
trying to dominate
trying to go all Fifty Shades of
                    Grey Owl

I laughed
shaking my head
môniyas, you so cute
that's adorable
you forget
I fuck Dene and Cree and Métis
men who fuck
like moose rut in September
dominant and on top
making me feel
soft and feminine and wild

they mark me
hickeys everywhere
tasting and devouring my body
until I beg for it
they are forever North
forever strong   forever free

môniyas, you spank me
and want me to call you Daddy
white guilt and privilege
narrow in your eyes
you wanna talk dirty to me
like they do in the pornos
never understanding
that my power
is beyond your slippery hands

you're an okay story
I'll play submissive for you
acting shy and shit
but I'm already thinking
of the next time
I get to break bannock
with a beautiful brown man

#612

he is
a white buffalo
this indigenous man

he stands tall
braid flowing down his back
his language on his tongue
and no hickeys
on his neck
no claims
on that territory

he is in boardrooms
sporting a suit and tie
he is on the land
ready with rifle and tobacco

he is paying his own bills
in his own house
via his own wifi
in his own sweet
pre-colonial time

he cooks moose meat stew
and reads books
he holds your hand
and two-steps across dance floors

he is
a white buffalo
an indigenous love
still hunting for that hickey
that forever sweetie
to stand by his side

#501

he spoke Halq'eméylem
breath tripping over
smooth tongue
licking his lips
smiling with ancestors
as language and tradition
surged through

I watched him
the way hunters watch a deer
slow and careful
breathing light
stepping softly
readying my bow
adjusting my breasts
licking my own lips

we circled one another
making eyes
grinning
waiting for the first to falter
the first to fall
the first to admit defeat

the expression
on his face
when he
stumbled
into the man-
trap

then I let him in
taking down
this exotic brown
with a grin
developing a taste
for salmon-raised men

#509

môniyas
I let you in
let you past
bedroom door
black lace underwear
deep inside

making love
chest to chest
lips and tongue mating
as we did
sweat dripping
laughter low
sweet wave of orgasm
clenching tight
holding you within

môniyas
I let you in
to my home
to my thoughts
to my heart
letting that feeling begin
you know that feeling
he could be special
this could be something
I like him
shit

making plans
in my head
of what this could mean
this political and social choice
of dating white
in a world of Indian Acts
and secondary citizenship
in a government system
designed to erase my rights
acknowledging that if I move forward with this
    feeling
I am assisting the colonized system

yeah, call it a feeling

#308

her lips
were soft pillows
reminding me of
Sunday morning cuddles
and the first bite of fry bread

my first
girl kiss
upstairs in the bathroom
music pumping through the floor
bright lights and no shame
in the exploration of lips and tongue and taste

damn
I was feeling two-spirited that night
and intimidated as fuck
she kissed
like a fresh piece of moose meat
soft and rich
multiple layers
beneath candy gloss

she bit me
pulling away
drawing me in
and I remembered
the guy I had been trying downstairs
but he don't kiss like this
like my mouth is his sacred space
his to devour
his to tempt
so I fall
a bit
deeper
down the rabbit hole

#912

I loved you
deeply and without reservation
I loved the way you spoke Dene
the way you respected your mama
the way you held my hand
the way you nibbled my ear

I loved you beneath northern lights
deep within boreal forests
I loved you in that old rusty car
I loved you in your new SUV

I loved you during late night convos
and a million texts
I loved you when that cell
got cut off

I loved you when you struggled
and I loved you when you chased your dreams
I loved you enough to say I do
and to give you family

I loved you
and you broke it

so now
awas
dénigha
to translate roughly:
get out of my sight
walk away and don't look back
I choose my path
you choose yours

#600

he's a little bit country
that twang in his voice
present even when he moans my name

his blue eyes and blond hair
are so clean
cut they hurt
and his lovemaking
is like vanilla ice cream and apple pie
or some other flavour
back in the day

he makes me believe
I could make him supper
knit by the fire
listen to his same old stories
pretend I don't like to be spanked
in the sack

he don't wanna hit a woman, you know

so we cuddle and he holds me close
murmuring nonsense as his strong arms
sweep around me gathering me in
smelling of man and sun and outdoors
farm fields and a hard day's work
he breathes deeply
head tipped back
kind of a hottie
even when snoring
down the place

typical
it is so me
easing out of his arms
shaking my head
stealing away

#602

I want to make him tremble
with desire
with lust
coursing through his blood
watch his breath hitch
as my nails graze soft spots
and my mouth
kisses sucks bites
neck shoulders lips

Instead
his blond hair
    falls between us
a hidden grin on his face
as he makes me
moan and hiss
arch and whimper
I just can't stop
he plays my entire body
with so much fingering

my hands shake
my hips rotate
losing control
the second he leans down
and I feel his smile
against my neck
as
he
starts
all
over
again

#608

in one glance
in one nod
you shelved me
in that dirty little section
between Squaw and Slut
because pure sexuality
was too broad a concept for you

so the problem
must have been me
and my oral ways
as opposed to you
and your systematic suppression

I stand up
tall and proud
sensuality in the pout of my lips
the curve of my hips
the swell of my breasts
and I smile

judge me all that you want
môniyas
I enjoy being woman
being sexual
being free
to claim my own partners
to crack up in bed
to throw back my head with laughter
to find joy
between sheets
under stars
within him
him and him
whoever I want

I am not your Pocahontas
your naughty squaw
your brown baby
your redskin lover
I am nothing to you
you are nothing to me

I define my sexuality
I define my boundaries
I decide
who I take into my bed
into my mouth
into my body
into my heart

I decide
not you

so judge me
when I laugh and smile
toss my hair back
two-stepping with your friends
leaning close and smelling that smell
lacing my fingers together
with tonight's sweetie

judge me
I dare you

#821

feelings are a mistake
making me think
that you were something more
than a good story

feelings got me all twisted
like I wanna make you fried bannock
pour you some thick golden syrup
to lick from my fingers

feelings got me waiting for your text
waiting for your smile
waiting
and baby, I ain't the waiting type

feelings got me thinking
I could live eight hours away
do the long distance thing
work my ass off
to see you more

feelings got me sitting here
smiling at nothing
while you don't even know
I've got a crush on you

fuck feelings
fuck them
right out

#325

big dick dene
dumb as fuck
hot as can be
isn't that always the case
those lips can lie and cheat and steal
telling me nothing
but what I wanna hear

still making me grin
those eyes are dene
dark and black
bringing back treaty nights
and status babies
and not to hit you
over the head with it
             but wow
                that dick

we don't text
his spelling hurts
keeps me up at night
over the croaking of frogs
and the wind whistling
he whispers into my ear
teaching me dene
teaching me how to moan
bénahchulé nezu
eeee

dene love
big dick dene lust
here's to keeping it real

bénahchulé nezu: I like your nice dick (Dene)

#903

you poured
dark molasses
onto pink nipples
letting it drip down
licking thick sweetness
from my flesh

I fed you bites
of fry bread
still warm and fresh
this is my body
my spirit
my laughter

babe
you crazy
making the sheets sticky
your hands pulling smoothing
kneading me into dessert
feasting upon pleasure
and moans of joy

you licked me clean
lapping up the sugar between my legs
mixed with the syrup of the North
two delicious solitudes
making me moan for ancestral strength
as I crested waves filled with visions
of lust and love and
pleasure

baby
I am slow to become
unstuck

#504

that first moment
when you see familiar brown
skin
lips
hands
and you see yourself
inside of him

that instant
when you wonder
if he understands
words like *nôkum* and *setsun*é
eats whitefish and moose meat
sleeps on living room floors
and knows the struggle of snagging
the best mink blanket in the house

those first few seconds
when you decide
hunter or gatherer
drummer or singer
if he uses his hands to chop wood
or to skin a moose
if he has ever ridden in a skiff
or if he has a old eland

that flirting glance
over your shoulder
tucking your hair behind your ear
smiling but not too much

in that moment
when he looks up
and smiles back

nôkum: my grandma (Cree)
*setsun*é: my grandma (Dene)

#692

I'm going back to my roots
I'm searching for that brown sweetie
who flirts like a boy from the Rez
shy and teasing
with a sly grin and a head nod
     that's a love nod
          you know

I'm looking for that
hand-holding hickey wearing
kind of man
who will spend his Treaty five on you
who will save you that last dry meat
who will smile and duck his head
laughing quiet
making you lean in
to share his joy

I'm looking for that man
who burns grass in the spring
chops wood in the summer
ice-fishes in the winter
ands moose in the fall
keeps you safe and well-fed
all year long

I'm looking for that sweet tanned man
who speaks his tradition in bed
who laughs too loud
and makes everyone around him
feel like his best friend

I'm looking for that
sweet and flirty and hot as fuck
indigenous love

acknowledgments

This is for the storytellers in my life.

For my parents, Isidore and Ornella Campbell, for always talking to my brothers and me, sharing laughter and joy, and allowing us the space and guidance to learn how to express ourselves.

For my Aunt Sharon, for gifting me with my first typewriter.

For my Auntie Millie and my friend Bonnie Yew, who translated the Dene and Cree for me amidst late night phone calls and laughter.

For all my Aunties who listened to me, teased me, and led the way.

about the author

Tenille Campbell is a Dene/Métis author and photographer from English River First Nation in Northern Saskatchewan. She completed her MFA in Creative Writing at UBC and is currently starting her fourth year of PhD studies at the University of Saskatchewan, focusing on Indigenous Literature.

She is the owner and artist behind *sweetmoon photography*, a successful photography business that specializes in photographing Indigenous people. She has published poetry in *Sing: Poetry from the Indigenous Americas*, and photography in *Urban Tribes: Native Americans in the City* and *Dreaming in Indian*.

Current creative projects include #KissingIndigenous, a photography series focusing on the act of intimacy within Indigenous couples. She is also the creator of tea&bannock, an online collective blog featuring the photographs and stories of Indigenous women photographers throughout Canada.

Storytelling — be it with ink, voice or photographs — is the life for her.

Eco-Audit
Printing this book using Rolland Enviro 100 Book
instead of virgin fibres paper saved the following resources:

Solid Waste	Water	Air Emissions
22 kg	1,816 L	204 kg